STONE
STACKING

A POCKET GUIDE

RP Minis™
Hachette Book Group
1290 Avenue of the Americas,
New York, NY 10104
www.runningpress.com
@Running_Press

First Edition: April 2020

Published by RP Minis, an imprint of Perseus Books, LLC, a subsidiary of Hachette Book Group, Inc. The RP Minis name and logo is a trademark of the Hachette Book Group.

The publisher is not responsible for websites (or their content) that are not owned by the publisher.

ISBN: 978-0-7624-6954-3

CONTENTS

INTRODUCTION

Whether you're looking for a way to pass the time, a distraction from social media, or a simple meditation exercise to center your mind, body, and spirit, stone stacking can prove to be just the soothing source of inspiration and calm you've been searching for.

Ready to rock? Read on to learn more about the ancient art of stone stacking.

WHY STONE STACKING?

Used widely across the globe as a meditative practice, stone stacking has grown in popularity in recent years. Maybe you've seen the Instagram-famous neon rocks in Nevada, called Seven Magic Mountains, or the photo-ready fixtures on Coachella's campgrounds, or maybe your local spa has an assortment of soothing stone arrangements nestled in the corner to aid in relaxation.

Either way, the sometimes artform, sometimes spiritual activity is here to stay, and for good reason. By stacking stones one on top of the other, held together only by the Earth's gravitational pull, many spiritualists find the serenity and sense of balance they seek. But there are many other reasons why one might choose to practice stone stacking. While some believe in the mindfulness and meditation the practice brings, others simply enjoy the value of creating a work of art using only natural materials. Still, some love the challenge that comes from finding the perfect balance between each stone. Whether it's in the wild or within the comforts of your own home, stone stacking can serve as a source of inspiration and fun for anyone.

A LITTLE HISTORY

Some believe stone stacking dates back to ancient Gaelic celebrations in which stones were stacked to celebrate the equinox and measure the sun for the solstice. The Gaelic tradition, known as Cairn, translates literally to *stack of stones*.

Cairns were commonly used to mark trails and mazes, helping passersby navigate unknown areas or travelers find their way back home.

Other functions included burial monuments, ceremonial spaces, defense against invaders, and hunting. The most famous example of a Cairn existing today? Stonehenge! The UNESCO site and stone stacking mecca is still standing in the English countryside. The prehistoric property was thought to be used for the funeral practices and solstice celebrations of peoples inhabiting the land as early as 3000 BC.

In the US, historians have found instances of stone stacks used by Native Americans as spiritual symbols, burial grounds, or markers indicating a natural feature like a river bed or spring. They've even uncovered an old farm in the Catskill Mountains that's home to an impressive stone stack they believe was once used (a staggering 4,500 years ago!) to mark the Big Dipper.

Despite having a place throughout history, modern government doesn't approve of stacking stones in the wild. The United States Parks Service has banned stone stacking while inside national parks. Why? Some environmentalists fear the shifting of stones (big or small) could affect the life quality of local flora and fauna. To be safe, stick to stacking the stones in this kit in your home or on a desktop.

You'll reap the same rewarding benefits and avoid any unwanted wildlife interference.

THE BENEFITS OF STONE STACKING

When practiced regularly, stone stacking can provide the same soothing outcome as a yoga class or meditation session. It requires the same sense of patience, focus, and stillness of mind you need to perfect your pose or channel your energy. But that's not where the benefits stop; there are plenty of other rewards stone stackers have acquired while building their latest and greatest stack.

GET SPIRITUAL. Many see stone stacking as a source of enlightenment or spirituality. A common practice is to choose smooth, natural pebbles, align an intention, prayer, or source of gratitude with each stone, and stack them one on top of the other. Maybe you want to stack a stone for all the people, places, and things that bring you joy. That means your stone stack intentions could be made up of the names of loved ones, your favorite travel destinations, or hobbies and hopes for your future. Every month, week, or day you can set a new intention for your stack and start fresh.

BOOST YOUR CREATIVITY.

Finding just the right position for each and every stone requires a touch of creativity and problem solving. By using some of your senses, like sight and touch, you'll be able to identify which stones will likely stack and stay balanced on one another.

TAKE A MUCH-NEEDED BREAK. Stone stacking requires your full attention and intense concentration—meaning your brain won't have time to process any other stress. Bye bye, nagging work emails, appointments, and anxiety-driven thoughts and fears. Hello, clear and content mind. By zeroing in on the task at hand (carefully stacking one stone on another and keeping them stable), you won't have time to let the worries of the everyday creep in.

MAKE YOUR OWN MASTERPIECE. Globally, stone stacking has become somewhat of a performance art phenomenon. There are yearly competitions where balancing artists from all over the world compete for the top spot and social media stars spend their days in

search of the next 'gram-worthy stone structure to strike a pose in front of.

START STACKING

Now that you know a little bit about the history and benefits behind stone stacking, it's time to start your own stack! First, you'll want to set a solid foundation using sand. Once you've layered your gritty base, add a large stone or boulder on top to start your stack. The goal is to keep your stones held together by nothing other than gravity. Stone stacking is about trial and error. View your stone stacking as a journey, not just an outcome.

While creativity is highly encouraged in the art of stone stacking, there are a few basic styles to help everyone from the novice stacker to the master boulder builder get their stack started. Here are four simple and popular techniques to try:

BALANCED STACKING:

rocks are laid flat upon
each other from biggest
to smallest at the apex

CLASSIC BALANCE:

each rock is balanced in
line with the previous

COUNTERBALANCE:

lower rocks depend on the
weight of the higher rocks
to maintain stability

FREESTYLE:
a combination of two of the above

———

Unlike many other forms of art (painting, drawing, sculpting), a mistake can be erased at a moment's notice. Unhappy with the way you've stacked your stones? Reset and try again. The most beautiful part of using this medium is the temporary nature of it. In fact, dedicated stone stacking artists often find the destruction of the stack to be as meaningful as building the stack itself. It allows them to start their creative process over and over again.

No matter your reasoning for stone stacking, let the healing and mind-balancing benefits soak in and quiet your doubts, fears, and worries. Whenever you feel a pang of stress or uncertainty strike, turn to your kit and start

stacking. Before you know it, you'll have reached a serene sense of Zen without stepping foot outside of your office or home. Happy stacking!

This book has been bound using handcraft methods and Smyth-sewn to ensure durability.

Written by Christine Kopaczewski.

Photo credits © GettyImages
p. 4: WachiraKhurimon, p. 6: Freeze-FrameStudio, p. 10: aroundtheworld photography, p. 16: MashaDodo, p. 24: People Images, p. 30: imagedepotpro

Designed by Amanda Richmond.